Student Pilot Guide FAA

FOREWORD

The Federal Aviation Administration (FAA) invites you to join the general aviation community of pilots. It is a community of civil aviation operations other than those air carriers holding a Certificate of Public Convenience and Necessity. General aviation makes up approximately 96 percent of U.S. aircraft and 60 percent of U.S. flight hours flown. General aviation is often misunderstood as only small, propeller-driven aircraft. A large jet or cargo plane operated under Title 14 of the Code of Federal Regulations (14 CFR) part 91 can be a general aviation aircraft.

This publication is intended to serve as a guide for prospective student pilots and for those already engaged in flight training. This guide presents in "how to" fashion, general procedures for obtaining FAA student pilot, sport pilot, recreational pilot, and private pilot certificates.

There are many references to FAA Flight Standards District Offices (FSDOs) and through the FSDOs, contact is maintained between the FAA and the general aviation public. The FAA inspectors at your local FSDO are professionally trained and are prepared to advise and assist you toward reaching your goal as a pilot.

FAA-H-8083-27A supersedes FAA-H-8083-27, Student Pilot Guide, dated 1999.

This handbook may be purchased from the Superintendent of documents, U.S. Government Printing Office (GPO), Washington DC 20402-9325, or from GPO's web site.

This handbook is published by the U.S. Department of Transportation, Federal Aviation Administration, Airman Testing Standards Branch, AFS-630, P.O. Box 25082, Oklahoma City, OK 73125-0082.

Comments regarding this publication should be sent, in e-mail form, to AFS630comments@faa.gov.

We urge you to visit your local FSDO and feel free to ask for advice on any matters relating to general aviation.

Welcome to aviation.

/s/ 3/8/2006
_____

Joseph K. Tintera, Manager,
Regulatory Support Division
Flight Standards Service

CONTENTS

INTRODUCTION
Role of the FAA 1
Flight Standards District Offices (FSDOs) 1
Most Frequently Asked Questions 1
Choosing a Flight School 2
The Role of the Instructor 3
What Flight Training Requires 3
Instructor and Student Relationship 4
Medical Requirements 4
Knowledge Tests 5
Preparing to Study for the Knowledge Test 5
Study Materials 6
Suggested Study Materials 6
How to Obtain Study Materials 6
How to Study for the Knowledge Test 7
Study Habits 8
When to Take the Knowledge Test 8
Where to Take the Knowledge Test 8
The Knowledge Test Content and Format 9
Practical Test Standards 9

MOST FREQUENTLY ASKED QUESTIONS
General 10
Student Pilot Flight Training 11
Student Pilot Requirements: Medical and Student
 Pilot Certificates 14
Sport Pilot, Recreational Pilot, and Private Pilot
 Knowledge Tests 18
Sport Pilot, Recreational Pilot, and Private Pilot
 Practical Tests 21

INTRODUCTION

Before you begin flight training, it is important to have a basic understanding of the responsibilities, safety regulations, and issues applicable to such an endeavor. This includes the choice of a flight school, selected study materials, study habits, and the role of the instructor, student, and Federal Aviation Administration (FAA).

Role of the FAA

Congress empowered the FAA to foster aviation safety by prescribing safety standards for civil aviation. This is accomplished through the Code of Federal Regulations (CFRs).

Title 14 of the Code of Federal Regulations (14 CFR) part 61 pertains to the certification of pilots, flight instructors, and ground instructors. This prescribes the eligibility, aeronautical knowledge, flight proficiency, and experience required for each type of pilot certificate issued.

Flight Standards District Offices (FSDOs)

Throughout the world, the FAA has approximately 100 Flight Standards District Offices and International Field Offices, commonly referred to as "FSDOs" and "IFOs." Through these offices, information and services are provided for the aviation community. In the U.S., FSDO phone numbers are listed in the blue pages of the telephone directory under United States Government Offices, Department of Transportation, Federal Aviation Administration. Another convenient method is using the FSDO Locator available on the Regulatory Support Division's web site.

http://www.faa.gov/about/office_org/headquarters_offices/avs/offices/afs/afs600

Most Frequently Asked Questions

The *Most Frequently Asked Questions* section on page 10 of this guide, lists typical questions, with answers, asked by student pilots. If your question is not answered, we suggest that you contact your local FSDO. The FSDO will be able to furnish current information regarding changes in procedures or revisions to regulations.

Choosing a Flight School

Most airports have facilities for flight training conducted by flight schools or individual flight instructors. A school will usually provide a wide variety of training material, special facilities, and greater flexibility in scheduling. Many colleges and universities also provide flight training as a part of their curricula.

There are two types of flight schools catering to primary general aviation needs. One is normally referred to as a certificated "part 141 school" and the other as a "part 61 school." A part 141 school has been granted an Air Agency Certificate by the FAA. The certificated schools may qualify for a ground school rating and a flight school rating. In addition, the school may be authorized to give their graduates practical (flight) tests and knowledge (computer administered written) tests. AC 140-2HH, FAA Certificated Pilot Schools Directory, lists certificated ground and flight schools and the pilot training courses each school offers. For ordering information, refer to the *How to Obtain Study Materials* section on page 6 of this guide. Another convenient method is through the Internet at the FAA's Regulatory and Guidance Library web site.

http://www.airweb.faa.gov/Regulatory_and_Guidance_Library/rgAdvisoryCircular.nsf/

Enrollment in a certificated school usually ensures quality and continuity of training. These schools meet prescribed standards with respect to equipment, facilities, personnel, and curricula. Many excellent flight schools find it impractical to qualify for the FAA part 141 certificate and are referred to as part 61 schools. One difference between a part 141 school and a part 61 school is that fewer flight hours are required to qualify for a pilot certificate in a part 141 certificated school. The requirement for a private pilot certificate is 40 hours in a part 61 school and 35 hours in a part 141 certificated school. This difference may be insignificant for a private pilot certificate because the national average indicates most pilots require 60 to 75 hours of flight training.

The FSDO will provide information on the location of pilot training facilities in your area. A current file is maintained on all schools within each FSDO's district. You make the decision on where to obtain flight training. You may want to make a checklist of things to look for in a school. Talking to pilots and reading articles in flight magazines can help you in making your checklist and in the evaluation of a training facility.

Your choice of a flight school might depend on whether you are planning to obtain a sport pilot certificate, recreational pilot certificate, private pilot certificate, or whether you intend to pursue a career as a professional pilot. Another consideration is whether you will train part time or full time.

Do not make the mistake of making your determination based on financial concerns alone. The quality of training you receive is very important. Prior to making a final decision, visit the school you are considering, and talk with management, instructors, and students. Evaluate the items on the checklist you developed, and then take time to think things over before making your decision.

Ground and flight training should be obtained as regularly and frequently as possible. This assures maximum retention of instruction and the achievement of requisite proficiency.

The Role of the Instructor

The student pilot's training program depends upon the quality of the ground and flight training received. An instructor should possess an understanding of the learning process, a knowledge of the fundamentals of teaching, and the ability to communicate effectively with the student pilot. During the certification process, a flight instructor applicant is tested on a practical application of these skills in specific teaching situations. The quality of instruction, and the knowledge and skills acquired from your flight instructor will affect your entire flying career whether you plan to pursue it as a vocation or an avocation.

What Flight Training Requires

A course of instruction should include the ground and flight training necessary to acquire the knowledge and skills required to safely and efficiently function as a certificated pilot. Whether you attend a part 141 or part 61 school or obtain the services of an individual flight instructor, the specific knowledge and skill areas for each category and class of aircraft are outlined in Title 14 of the Code of Federal Regulations (14 CFR). Refer to 14 CFR part 61, subpart J for the requirements of a sport pilot certificate. Refer to 14 CFR part 61, subpart D for the requirements of a recreational pilot certificate. Refer to 14 CFR part 61, subpart E for the requirements of a private pilot certificate.

Instructor and Student Relationship

The FAA has adopted an operational training concept that places the full responsibility for student training on the flight instructor. In this role, the flight instructor assumes total responsibility for training you to meet the standards required for certification within an ever-changing operating environment.

Like anything else in life, the more you educated yourself and are aware of what is expected of you and others, the more control you have of your goal's outcome. Research the avenues open to you. Get impartial opinions of the flight school and/or instructor you intend to employ.

The flight instructor will provide you guidance, and arrange for your academic and flight training lessons. These lessons are presented in a logical manner to achieve desired goals. After each flight, the flight instructor will review the day's lesson. This will be the time to clear up any questions. It is important that misconceptions be clarified while the subject is still fresh in mind.

Medical Requirements

Pilots, except those who fly gliders or free air balloons, must possess a valid medical certificate in order to exercise the privileges of their airman certificates. Sport pilots must possess either a valid third-class medical certificate or a valid driver's license.

The periodic medical examination required for medical certification is conducted by designated aviation medical examiners, who are physicians with a special interest in aviation safety and have training in aviation medicine.

The standards for medical certification are contained in 14 CFR part 67. The requirements for obtaining medical certification are contained in 14 CFR part 61.

Prior to beginning flight training, a flight instructor should interview you about any health conditions and determine your goal as a pilot. Good advice would be to obtain the class of medical certificate required, for the certificate level you ultimately want, before beginning flight training. Finding out immediately whether you are medically qualified could save time and money.

If you do have physical limitations, such as impaired vision, loss of a limb, or hearing impairment it is possible you could be issued a medical certificate valid for "Student Pilot Privileges Only." This kind of medical certificate will allow you to continue flight training and to prepare for the pilot certification practical test. During training, flight instructors should ensure that you can safely perform all required TASKs that pertain to the required standards. Special devices may be necessary to allow you to manipulate the flight controls. If you are unable to perform certain TASKs, you may have a limitation placed on your pilot certificate. For example, hearing impairment would require the limitation "Not Valid for Flight Requiring the Use of Radio." Another limitation may allow the pilot to only operate a certain make and model airplane, such as one without rudder pedals.

Knowledge Tests

Communication between individuals through the use of words is a complicated process. In addition to being an exercise in the application and use of aeronautical knowledge, a knowledge test is also an exercise in communication since it involves the use of written language. Since the tests involve written rather than spoken words, communication between the test writer and the person being tested may become a difficult matter if both parties do not exercise care. For this reason, considerable effort is expended to write each question in a clear, precise manner.

Preparing to Study for the Knowledge Test

Your instructor will direct you to the textbooks and other sources of training and testing materials that are available from the Superintendent of Documents, U.S. Government Printing Office, and the Regulatory Support Division's web site.

http://www.faa.gov/about/office_org/headquarters_offices/avs/offices/afs/afs600

Your instructor may use commercial publications as a source of study materials, and these materials may be desirable, especially for aircraft categories where government materials are limited.

Study Materials

The FAA develops and makes available to the public various sources of aeronautical information. Some of this information is free; other information is available at a nominal cost. Of particular interest and value to those persons getting started in flying are: FAA-H-8083-27A, Student Pilot Guide; FAA-H-8083-3, Airplane Flying Handbook; FAA-H-8083-25, Pilot's Handbook of Aeronautical Knowledge; Aeronautical Information Manual (AIM); and Practical Test Standards (PTSs). In addition, many aviation publications are available from commercial sources.

Suggested Study Materials

- 14 CFR parts 1, 61, 67, and 91
- Aeronautical Information Manual
- AC 00-6, Aviation Weather
- AC 00-45, Aviation Weather Services
- FAA-H-8083-1, Pilot's Weight and Balance
- FAA-H-8083-3, Airplane Flying Handbook
- FAA-H-8083-11, Balloon Flying Handbook
- FAA-H-8083-13, Glider Flying Handbook
- FAA-H-8083-21, Rotorcraft Flying Handbook
- FAA-H-8083-25, Pilot's Handbook of Aeronautical Knowledge
- FAA-S-8081-3, Recreational Pilot Practical Test Standards
- FAA-S-8081-14, Private Pilot Practical Test Standards (Airplane)
- FAA-S-8081-29, Sport Pilot Practical Test Standards (Airplane, Gyroplane, Glider and Flight Instructor)
- FAA-S-8081-30, Sport Pilot Practical Test Standards (Airship, Balloon, and Flight Instructor)
- FAA-S-8081-31, Sport Pilot Practical Test Standards (Weight Shift Control, Powered Parachute, and Flight Instructor)
- FAA-S-8081-32, Private Pilot Practical Test Standards (Powered Parachute and Weight Shift Control)
- www.faasafety.gov

How to Obtain Study Materials

The current Flight Standards Service airman training and testing material and questions banks for all airman certificates and ratings can be obtained from the Regulatory Support Division's web site.

http://www.faa.gov/about/office_org/headquarters_offices/avs/offices/afs/afs600

AC 00-2, Advisory Circular Checklist, transmits the status of all FAA advisory circulars (ACs), as well as FAA internal publications and miscellaneous flight information, such as Aeronautical Information Manual, Airport/Facility Directory, practical test standards, and other material directly related to a certificate or rating. AC 00-2 is accessible through the Internet at the following address.

http://www.faa.gov/aba/html_policies/ac00-2.html

The Airport/Facility Directory and Aeronautical Charts are available on a subscription or one time basis from the following:

U.S. Department of Transportation
Federal Aviation Administration
National Aeronautical Charting Office Distribution Center
Greenbelt, MD 20770-1479
1-800-638-8972
http://www.naco.faa.gov

The National Transportation Safety Board Regulation Part 830 is available free of charge from the following:

National Transportation Safety Board
ATTN: Public Inquiry
490 L'Enfant Plaza East, S.W.
Washington, DC 20594.

Most airport fixed base operators and flight schools carry a variety of Government publications and charts, as well as commercially published materials.

How to Study for the Knowledge Test

You should follow your instructor's advice on what and when to study. You should recognize the advantages of planning a definite study program and following it as closely as possible. Haphazard or disorganized study habits usually result in an unsatisfactory score on the knowledge test.

The ideal study program is to enroll in a formal ground school course. This offers the advantages of a school with professional instructors, as well as facilities and training aids designed for pilot instruction. Many of these schools use audiovisual aids to supplement classroom instruction or provide individual computer-based instruction.

For the applicant who is unable to attend a school, the self-study method can be satisfactory, provided the proper study materials are obtained, and a reasonable amount of time is devoted to study. The applicant should establish realistic periodic goals, and equally important, a target date for completion. Self-discipline is important because it is too easy to "put off" the study period for some other activity.

Study Habits
The use of a training syllabus is an effective way for the flight instructor to lead you through the proper steps in learning to fly safely.

When beginning flight training, the development of good study habits includes the practice of visualizing the flight instructor's explanation plus those of the textbook.

Study habits should include time spent with cockpit familiarization. This includes reviewing checklists, identifying controls, and learning the cockpit arrangement.

When to Take the Knowledge Test
Experience has shown that the knowledge test is more meaningful to the applicant, and is more likely to result in a satisfactory grade, if it is taken after beginning the flight portion of the training. For optimum benefit, it is recommended that the knowledge test be taken after the student has completed a solo cross-country flight. The operational knowledge gained by this experience can be used to the student's advantage in the knowledge test. Your instructor will be the best indicator of your preparedness for the test.

Where to Take the Knowledge Test
FAA-Designated Computer Testing Centers have been certificated to administer FAA knowledge tests. Applicants will be charged a fee for the administration of FAA knowledge tests. Test registration numbers and a complete list of test centers can be downloaded from the Regulatory Support Division's web site.

http://www.faa.gov/about/office_org/headquarters_offices/avs/offices/afs/afs600

Contact your local FSDO to obtain information concerning an FAA-Designated Computer Testing Center in your area.

Note: If you are enrolled in a part 141 school with test examining authority, the school will administer the knowledge test during the curriculum.

The Knowledge Test Content and Format

The knowledge test contains questions of the objective, multiple-choice type. This testing method conserves the applicant's time, eliminates any element of individual judgment in determining grades, and saves time in scoring.

Practical Test Standards

The flight proficiency maneuvers listed in 14 CFR part 61 are the standard skill requirements for certification. They are outlined in the practical test standards (PTSs) as "AREAS OF OPERATION." These AREAS OF OPERATION are phases of the practical test arranged in a logical sequence within the standard. They begin with "Preflight Preparation" and end with "Postflight Procedures." Roman numerals preceding each AREA OF OPERATION relate to the corresponding AREAS OF OPERATION contained in the regulation.

Each AREA OF OPERATION contains "TASKs," which are comprised of knowledge areas, flight procedures, and/or flight maneuvers appropriate to the AREA OF OPERATION. You are required to demonstrate knowledge and proficiency in ALL TASKs for the original-issuance of all pilot certificates.

You should obtain a copy of the practical test standard appropriate to the pilot certificate that you plan to acquire. This will enable you to know exactly what is expected on the practical test. Practical test standards can be obtained from the Regulatory Support Division's web site.

http://www.faa.gov/about/office_org/headquarters_offices/avs/offices/afs/afs600

MOST FREQUENTLY ASKED QUESTIONS

General

1. Q. Is it difficult to fly an aircraft?

A. *No. It is not particularly difficult. As a beginning student pilot, you will do most of the actual flying (handling the controls of the aircraft).*

2. Q. When may I begin to fly?

A. *Immediately. However, you will need to apply for certain certificates, as described in this guide, in preparation for solo flight.*

3. Q. Is flying safe?

A. *A well-built and maintained aircraft, flown by a competent and prudent pilot, makes flying as safe or safer than many other forms of transportation.*

4. Q. If engine failure occurs, what will happen?

A. *Modern aircraft engines are very reliable, and complete engine failure is a rare occurrence. If the improbable does happen, you will not "fall out of the sky." Just do what the instructor had you practice during lessons—select a good landing area and land.*

Student Pilot Flight Training

1. Q. What are the eligibility requirements for a student pilot?

A. The specific aeronautical experience requirements are outlined in 14 CFR part 61. For the student pilot certificate requirements, refer to subpart C section 83.

2. Q. Where can I obtain my ground and flight school training?

A. Most airport operators can furnish this information, or you may contact the nearest FSDO.

3. Q. Is there a set number of flight instructional hours I will receive before I solo?

A. No. The instructor will not allow you to solo until you have learned to perform certain maneuvers. These maneuvers include safe takeoffs and landings. You must be able to maintain positive control of the aircraft at all times and to use good judgment.

4. Q. What should I know about Title 14 of the Code of Federal Regulations (14 CFR) prior to my first solo?

A. Your flight instructor will determine that you are familiar with appropriate portions of 14 CFR part 61, the general and visual flight rules of 14 CFR part 91, and will administer and grade a presolo written test prior to solo endorsement. The presolo written test will also include questions on the flight characteristics and operational limitations of the make and model aircraft to be flown.

5. Q. What does an appropriate logbook endorsement for solo mean?

A. It means a verification by an authorized flight instructor showing that on the date specified, the student was given dual instruction and found competent to make solo flights.

6. Q. When is the first solo endorsement required?

A. A student pilot must have a first solo endorsement dated within 90 days prior to any solo flight.

7. Q. What is the difference between a recreational pilot certificate and a private pilot certificate?

A. The recreational pilot has fewer privileges than the private pilot. The holder of a recreational pilot certificate is allowed to fly an aircraft within 50 nautical miles from the airport where instruction was received and cannot operate in airspace where communications with air traffic control are required. Since qualification training in these areas is not required, a person should be able to obtain a recreational pilot certificate in fewer flight hours than required for a private pilot certificate. All privileges and limitations of the recreational pilot certificate are listed in 14 CFR part 61, section 101.

8. Q. Where can I get information about the Sport Pilot Program?

A. Sport pilot enthusiasts may find information on the Regulatory Support Division's web site at http://www.faa.gov/about/office_org/headquarters_offices/avs/offices/afs/afs600 in the Light Sport Aviation Branch's (AFS-610) area.

9. Q. Does a student pilot automatically have the privilege of cross-country flying after soloing?

A. No. An instructor must have reviewed the pilot's preflight planning and preparation for solo cross-country flight and determine that the flight can be made safely under the known circumstances and conditions. The instructor must endorse the student pilot's logbook prior to each cross-country flight, stating the pilot is considered competent to make the flight. Under certain conditions, an instructor may authorize repeated solo flights over a given route.

10. Q. As a student pilot, am I permitted to carry passengers prior to receipt of my recreational pilot certificate or private pilot certificate?

A. No.

11. Q. Must I have a Federal Communications Commission (FCC) radiotelephone operator's permit to operate an aircraft radio transmitter?

A. No.

12. Q. For the purpose of obtaining an additional certificate or rating, may the holder of a recreational pilot certificate act as pilot in command on flights: (1) between sunset and sunrise; and (2) in airspace which requires communication with air traffic control?

A. Yes, provided an authorized flight instructor has given the recreational pilot the required ground and flight training in these areas, and endorsed the pilot's logbook. The recreational pilot will be required to carry the logbook with the required endorsements on such flights.

13. Q. How can the holder of a sport or recreational pilot certificate ensure that no inadvertent entry is made into airspace requiring communication with air traffic control?

A. The pilot must select readily identifiable landmarks that are well beyond the boundaries of the airspace requiring communication with air traffic control. During training, instruction in identification of airspace requiring communication with air traffic control will be provided.

Student Pilot Requirements: Medical and Student Pilot Certificates

1. Q. When do I need a student pilot certificate?

A. Prior to solo flight.

2. Q. How do I obtain a student pilot certificate?

A. Student pilot certificates may be issued by an FAA Inspector or an FAA-Designated Pilot Examiner. Upon your request, a combination medical certificate and student pilot certificate will be issued by an FAA-Authorized Aviation Medical Examiner upon the satisfactory completion of your physical examination. Applicants who fail to meet certain requirements or who have physical disabilities, which might limit, but not prevent, their acting as pilots should contact their local FSDO.

3. Q. If I only want to be a sport pilot how do I obtain a student pilot certificate?

A. Sport pilot applicants who intend to fly without attaining a medical, but who will fly on the basis of a valid driver's license will only get a student pilot certificate issued by an FAA Inspector or FAA-Designated Pilot Examiner.

4. Q. If I have had a medical certificate denied can I just get a sport pilot certificate and fly on the basis of my driver's license?

A. No, The only way to fly as a sport pilot on the basis of a driver's license in lieu of a medical certificate is if your LAST FAA-medical was not denied.

5. Q. Where can I get more information about the sport pilot arena?

A. Sport pilot enthusiasts may find information on the Regulatory Support Division's web site at http://www.faa.gov/about/office_org/headquarters_offices/avs/offices/afs/afs600 in the AFS-610 area.

6. Q. What are the requirements for a student pilot certificate?

A. To be eligible for a student pilot certificate, a person must:

(1) be at least 16 years of age, except for the operation of a glider or balloon, in which case the applicant must be at least 14 years of age; and
(2) be able to read, speak, write, and understand the English language.

7. Q. How long are my student pilot and medical certificates valid?

A. The student pilot certificate will expire at the end of the 24th month after the month in which it was issued. The third-class medical certificate will expire at the end of the 36th month after the month in which it was issued. A medical certificate issued after the age of 40, expires at the end of the 24th month in which it was issued.

8. Q. Can my student pilot certificate be renewed?

A. No, but a new student pilot certificate may be issued by an:

(1) FAA-Authorized Aviation Medical Examiner, upon completion of the required examination; or
(2) FAA Inspector or FAA-Designated Pilot Examiner if you already hold a valid medical certificate or if you are not required to hold a medical certificate.

9. Q. If my original student pilot certificate has been endorsed for solo, do I lose this endorsement on my new certificate?

A. The endorsements are still valid, but are not transferred to the new certificate. Retain the old certificate as a record of these endorsements.

10. Q. Should my flight instructor endorse my student pilot certificate before or after my first solo flight?

A. The endorsement on the student pilot certificate certifying that the holder is competent to solo must be made by the flight instructor prior to the first solo flight.

11. Q. If I solo in more than one make and model aircraft, must I have an endorsement for each on my student pilot certificate?

A. Yes. Your flight instructor must make this endorsement prior to the first solo flight in each make and model aircraft.

12. Q. Does the endorsement to solo permit me to make solo cross-country flights?

A. No. Your flight instructor must specifically endorse your student pilot certificate to permit cross-country flights.

13. Q. Must I carry my student pilot certificate when I am piloting an aircraft in solo flight?

A. Yes. The certificate should be in your physical possession or readily accessible.

14. Q. Is there a charge for the student pilot certificate?

A. When the student pilot certificate is issued by a FSDO there is no charge. An FAA-Designated Pilot Examiner is allowed to charge a reasonable fee for issuing Student Pilot Certificates, and processing the necessary reports. The FAA-Authorized Aviation Medical Examiner will charge a fee for the physical examination in connection with issuing the combination medical and student pilot certificate.

15. Q. When do I need a medical certificate?

A. Except for sport pilot applicants, you will need a medical certificate prior to solo flight if you are operating an airplane, helicopter, gyroplane, or airship. It is suggested you obtain your medical certificate prior to beginning flight training. This will assure you are aware of any condition that could prevent you from obtaining a medical certificate prior to making a financial investment in flight training.

16. Q. If required, how do I get a medical certificate?

A. By passing a physical examination administered by a doctor who is an FAA-Authorized Aviation Medical Examiner.

17. Q. Where do I get my medical certificate?

A. From any FAA-Authorized Aviation Medical Examiner. There are numerous doctors who are FAA-Authorized Aviation Medical Examiners.

18. Q. Where can I get a list of FAA-Authorized Aviation Medical Examiners?

A. The FAA lists a directory on the Internet on the Civil Aeromedical Institute's web site.

www.faa.gov/pilots/amelocator/

19. Q. When required, what class of medical certificate must a student pilot have?

A. Third-class, although any class will suffice. Medical certificates are designated as first-class, second-class, or third-class. Generally, the first-class is designed for the airline transport pilot; the second-class for the commercial pilot; and the third-class for the student, recreational, and private pilot.

20. Q. If I have a physical disability, is there any provision for obtaining a medical certificate?

A. Yes. Medical certificates can be issued in many cases where physical disabilities are involved. Depending upon the certificate held and the nature of the disability, operating limitations may be imposed. If you have any questions, contact an FAA-Authorized Aviation Medical Examiner prior to beginning flight training.

21. Q. Must I have my medical certificate, when I am piloting an aircraft in solo flight?

A. Yes. The certificate should be in your physical possession or readily accessible.

Sport Pilot, Recreational Pilot, and Private Pilot Knowledge Tests

1. Q. What is the age requirement to take the sport pilot, recreational pilot, or private pilot knowledge test?

A. An applicant must be at least 15 years of age to take the test, although applicants for the balloon or glider tests must be 14 years of age. Prior to taking the knowledge test, an applicant shall be asked to present a birth certificate or other official documentation as evidence of meeting the age requirement.

2. Q. What aircraft can I fly as a sport pilot?

A. You are limited to flying an aircraft that meets the definition of a light-sport aircraft (LSA). An LSA is any certificated aircraft that meets the following performance parameters:

1,320 pounds Maximum Gross Weight (1,430 pounds for seaplanes)
45 knots (51 mph) Max Landing Configuration Stall
120 knots (138 mph) Max. Straight & Level
Single or Two seat Aircraft
Fixed Pitch or Ground Adjustable Propeller
Fixed Landing Gear (except for amphibious aircraft)

3. Q. What are the restrictions on a sport pilot?

A. Sport pilots cannot make flights:

- *at night;*
- *in controlled airspace unless you receive training and a logbook endorsement;*
- *outside the U.S. without advance permission from that country(ies);*
- *for the purpose of sight-seeing with passengers for charity fundraisers;*
- *above 10,000' MSL;*
- *when the flight or surface visibility is less than 3 statute miles;*
- *unless you can see the surface of the Earth for flight reference;*
- *in LSA with a maximum speed in level flight with maximum continuous power (V_h) of greater than 87 knots (100 mph), unless you receive training and a logbook endorsement;*
- *if the operating limitations issued with the aircraft do not permit that activity;*

- *contrary to any limitation listed on the pilot's certificate, U.S. driver's license, FAA medical certificate, or logbook endorsement(s); and*
- *while carrying a passenger or property for compensation or hire (no commercial operations).*

4. Q. How should I prepare for the knowledge test?

A. *To adequately prepare for the knowledge test, your instructor should review with you:*

(1) 14 CFR part 61, section 97 (if preparing for the recreational pilot knowledge test);
(2) 14 CFR part 61, section 105 (if preparing for the private pilot knowledge test); or
(3) 14 CFR part 61, section 309 (if preparing for the sport pilot knowledge test).

The regulations require an applicant to have logged ground training from an authorized instructor, or to present evidence of having satisfactorily completed a course of instruction or home-study course in the knowledge areas appropriate to the category and class aircraft for the rating sought.

5. Q. What document or documents must I present prior to taking a knowledge test?

A. *An applicant for a knowledge test must present appropriate personal identification. The identification must include a photograph of the applicant, the applicant's signature, and the applicant's actual residential address (if different from the mailing address). This information may be presented in more than one form. The applicant must also present one of the following:*

(1) A certificate of graduation from an FAA-approved pilot school or pilot training course appropriate to the certificate or rating sought, or a statement of accomplishment from the school certifying the satisfactory completion of the ground-school portion of such a course.
(2) A written statement or logbook endorsement from an FAA-Certificated Ground or Flight Instructor, certifying that the applicant has satisfactorily completed an applicable ground training or home-study course and is prepared for the knowledge test.

(3) A certificate of graduation or statement of accomplishment from a ground-school course appropriate to the certificate or rating sought conducted by an agency, such as a high school, college, adult education program, the Civil Air Patrol, or an ROTC Flight Training Program.

(4) A certificate of graduation from a home-study course developed by the aeronautical enterprise providing the study material. The certificate of graduation must correspond to the FAA knowledge test for the certificate or rating sought. The aeronautical enterprise providing the course of study must also supply a comprehensive knowledge test, which can be scored as evidence that the student has completed the course of study. When the student satisfactorily completes the knowledge test, it is sent to the course provider for scoring by an FAA-Certificated Ground or Flight Instructor. The instructor personally evaluates the test and attests to the student's knowledge of the subjects presented in the course. Upon satisfactory completion, a graduation certificate is sent to the student.

(5) In the event of retesting after a failure, the applicant must present the unsatisfactory Airman Test Report. If the applicant elects to retest for a higher score, the satisfactory Airman Test Report must be surrendered to the test administrator.

6. Q. If I fail the knowledge test, is there any way to determine the areas in which I need additional work, so I can study for a retest?

A. Yes. You will receive an Airman Test Report from the testing center. The test report will contain your test score and will also list topic and content descriptions for the areas in which you were deficient.

7. Q. If I pass the knowledge test, will I receive the same information concerning areas in which I need additional work as I would if I failed the test?

A. Yes. (Refer to the previous answer.)

8. Q. How long is a satisfactorily completed knowledge test valid?

A. 2 years. A satisfactorily completed knowledge test expires at the end of the day of the 24th month after the month in which it was taken. If a practical test is not satisfactorily completed during that period, another knowledge test must be taken.

Sport Pilot, Recreational Pilot, and Private Pilot Practical Tests

1. Q. Prior to taking the practical test, what aeronautical experience must I have?

A. *The specific aeronautical experience requirements are outlined in 14 CFR part 61.*

(1) 14 CFR 61, subpart J, section 313 for the sport pilot certificate requirements.
(2) 14 CFR part 61, subpart D, section 99 for the recreational pilot certificate requirements.
(3) 14 CFR part 61, subpart E, section 109 for the private pilot certificate requirements.

2. Q. Must I provide the aircraft for my practical test?

A. *Yes. An applicant must provide an airworthy aircraft with equipment relevant to the AREAS OF OPERATION required for the practical test.*

3. Q. What papers and documents must I present prior to my practical test?

A. *The applicant will be asked to present:*

(1) FAA Form 8710-1(8710.11 for sport pilot applicants), Application for an Airman Certificate and/or Rating, with the flight instructor's recommendation;
(2) an Airman Test Report with a satisfactory grade;
(3) a medical certificate (not required for glider or balloon), and a student pilot certificate endorsed by a flight instructor for solo, solo cross-country (airplane and rotorcraft), and for the make and model aircraft to be used for the practical test. (Drivers license or medical certificate for sport pilot applicants);
(4) the pilot log book records; and
(5) a graduation certificate from an FAA-approved school (if applicable).

The applicant will be asked to produce and explain the:

(1) aircraft's registration certificate;
(2) aircraft's airworthiness certificate;

(3) aircraft's operating limitations or FAA-approved aircraft flight manual (if required);
(4) aircraft equipment list;
(5) required weight and balance data;
(6) maintenance records; and
(7) applicable Airworthiness Directives.

4. Q. What pilot maneuvers are required on the practical test, and how will my performance of these operations be evaluated?

A. If a detailed explanation of the required pilot maneuvers and performance standards is desired, refer to either the sport pilot, recreational pilot, or private pilot practical test standards. The practical test standards may be downloaded free of charge from the Regulatory Support Division's web site http://www.faa.gov/about/office_org/headquarters_offices/avs/offices/afs/afs600 or purchased from the Superintendent of Documents or U.S. Government Printing Office bookstores. Refer to pages 6 and 7, of this guide, for directions

5. Q. What is the minimum age requirement for a sport pilot certificate, recreational pilot certificate, or private pilot certificate?

A. An applicant must be 17 years of age. Although, applicants for the private pilot glider or free balloon rating may be 16 years of age.

6. Q. When can I take the sport pilot, recreational pilot, or private pilot practical test?

A. 14 CFR part 61 establishes the ground school and flight experience requirements for the recreational pilot certificate and private pilot certificate. However, your flight instructor can best determine when your qualified for the practical test. Your instructor should take you through a practice practical test.

7. Q. Where can I take the practical test?

A. Due to the varied responsibilities of the FSDOs, practical tests are given by pilot examiners designated by FSDOs. You should schedule your practical test by an appointment to avoid conflicts and wasted time. A list of examiner names can be obtained from your local FSDO.

8. Q. Is there any charge for taking the practical test?

A. Since an FAA-Designated Pilot Examiner serves without pay from the government for conducting practical tests and processing the necessary reports, the FAA-Designated Pilot Examiner is allowed to charge a reasonable fee. However, there is no charge for the practical test when conducted by an FAA Inspector.

9. Q. May I exercise the privileges of my pilot certificate immediately after passing my practical test or must I wait until I receive the actual pilot certificate?

A. Yes. After satisfactory completion of the private pilot practical test, the examiner will issue you a temporary airman certificate. This is a valid certificate that authorizes you to exercise the privileges of a private pilot with appropriate ratings and/or limitations. This is an interim certificate issued subject to the approval of the Federal Aviation Administration pending the issuance of your permanent certificate. You normally will receive your permanent certificate within 120 days.

10. Q. Is there a charge for the pilot certificate?

A. No. There is no charge for any original certificate issued by the FAA. However, fees will be charged by the FAA-Authorized Aviation Medical Examiner for the medical examination and by the FAA-Designated Pilot Examiner for conducting the practical test. The FAA does charge to replace any pilot or medical certificate.

Made in the USA
Lexington, KY
17 February 2018